COFFEE COOK[illegible]K FOR BEGINNERS

Definitive Guide To Delicious Simple Coffee Recipes For Healthier Eating Without Skimping On Flavor

Luigi Russo

Let's start!

Table of Contents

7 Tips for Making Great Iced Coffee

Summer is finally upon us and most days are just too warm for hot cup of java juice. Below are some tips to help you make a great iced coffee.

1. Start with fresh coffee beans. A great iced coffee was never made using stale beans so avoid buying your beans on sale. If you don't drink iced coffee often, consider buying fresh beans at a coffee shop where you can buy only the amount you need for the occasion.

2. Test the taste. Hot coffee tastes different than cold coffee. So to get an idea of how your coffee will taste cold let a hot cup cool to room temperature. This little test will help you decide what tastes perfect to you.

3. Use fresh ice. Ice has a tendency to get a stale if it sits in the freezer unused for too long. If you're wondering whether your ice is helping of hurting your iced coffee, it's easy to test: let a few cubes melt and come to room temperature, then taste the resulting water. If it's water you would want to drink by the glassful, you're in good shape. If not, toss out the old ice and make fresh. If it still tastes stale, buy a bag of ice, the cost is worth the boost in flavor.

4. Brew it strong. Brew your coffee on the strong side as it will be weakened by the ice. To keep from diluting your drink, try turning your leftover coffee into ice cubes. Use these in the place of regular ice cubes to keep your drink chilled.

5. Try a cold brew. Some people object to acidity in their cold coffee. Cold brewing greatly reduces the acid content of coffee (with the same coffee it will lower the acidity one full pH point vs. hot brew). Put 3/4

cup ground coffee in a quart Mason jar, fill with water and stir. Cap it and put in the refrigerator for 12 hours. Strain the resulting concentrate through a coffee filter to remove the grinds. Add water to taste when you're ready to drink. You can even heat the reconstituted beverage for a quick, low-acid cup of hot coffee.

6. Don't use burned coffee for your iced coffee. Saving leftover coffee for iced beverage is often fine, but don't be tempted to use the dregs of a burnt pot. If it doesn't taste good hot, it definitely won't taste good cold.

7. Add some zip to your iced coffee. Adding fruits like strawberries, oranges, blueberries or even cherries and spices like nutmeg, cinnamon or cardamom are a great way to perk up your drink and your day. The important thing is to have fun with it! Try lots of new things. Vary your usual routine. The worst that can happen is you won't like it. You can always try something else!

If you're short on time and don't have a stash of reconstituted coffee available, try this recipe using instant coffee.

71 Delicious

Recipes

Mocha Coffee Mix

Ingredients

- 1 1/4 cups instant coffee granules
- 7 cups dry milk powder
- 5 3/4 cups powdered chocolate drink mix
- 1/4 cup confectioners' sugar
- 1 3/4 cups powdered non-dairy creamer

Directions

In a large bowl, mix together instant coffee, milk powder, chocolate drink mix, confectioners' sugar and powdered creamer. Store in an airtight container.

To serve, place 4 tablespoons of mixture into a coffee mug. Stir in 1 cup boiling water.

Raspberry Cream Cheese Coffee Cake

Ingredients

- 2 1/4 cups all-purpose flour 3/4 cup sugar
- 3/4 cup cold butter
- 1/2 teaspoon baking powder 1/2 teaspoon baking soda
  1/2 teaspoon salt
- 3/4 cup sour cream
- 1 egg, beaten
- 1 1/2 teaspoons almond extract FILLING:
- 1 (8 ounce) package cream cheese, softened
- 1/2 cup sugar 1 egg
- 1/2 cup raspberry jam
  1/2 cup slivered almonds

Directions

In a large mixing bowl, combine flour and sugar. Cut in butter until mixture is crumbly. Remove 1 cup and set aside. To the remaining crumbs, add baking powder, baking soda and salt.

Add the sour cream, egg and almond extract; mix well. Spread in the bottom and 2 in. up the sides of a greased 9-in. springform pan.

For the filling, in a small bowl, beat cream cheese, sugar and egg in a small bowl until blended. Pour over batter; spoon raspberry jam on top. Sprinkle with almonds and reserved crumbs.Bake at 350 degrees F for 55-60 minutes.

Let stand for 15 minutes Carefully run a knife around the edge of pan to loosen; remove sides from pan.

Coffee Liqueur III

Ingredients

- 1 1/2 cups white sugar
- 1 cup water
- 2 tablespoons instant coffee powder
- 1 teaspoon vanilla extract
- 20 fluid ounces vodka

Directions

Put white sugar, water, instant coffee, and vanilla extract in a 2 quart saucepan and bring to a boil. Simmer 5 minutes.

Put coffee mixture in fridge to cool. When cool, skim off scum and add vodka, stir and pour into bottles.

Coffee-Drizzled Cream Cheese Pie

Ingredients

- 1 (8 ounce) package PHILADELPHIA Cream Cheese, softened
- 1/3 cup sugar
- 1/2 cup milk
- 2 tablespoons GENERAL FOODS INTERNATIONAL Suisse Mocha Cafe
- 1 (8 ounce) tub COOL WHIP Whipped Topping, thawed
- 1 HONEY MAID Graham Pie Crust

Directions

Beat cream cheese in medium bowl until creamy. Gradually add sugar, mixing until well blended. Stir in milk. Remove 1/4 cup of the cream cheese mixture; place in small bowl. Stir in flavored instant coffee mix. Drizzle 1 Tbsp. of the coffee-flavored cream cheese mixture onto bottom of crust. Set remaining flavored cream cheese mixture aside.

Stir whipped topping gently into remaining plain cream cheese mixture, stirring just until marbleized. Spoon into crust. Drizzle with remaining coffee-flavored cream cheese mixture. Swirl knife gently through mixtures several times for marble effect.

Refrigerate 2 hours or until set. Store leftover pie in refrigerator.

Jill's World-Famous Coffee Liqueur Brownies

Ingredients

- 8 (1 ounce) squares unsweetened chocolate
- 1 cup butter
- 5 eggs
- 3 cups white sugar
- 1 tablespoon vanilla extract
- 1 1/2 cups all-purpose flour
- 1/2 cup coffee flavored liqueur
- 2 cups chopped walnuts

Directions

Preheat the oven to 375 degrees F (190 degrees C). Grease a 9x13 inch baking pan. In a heavy saucepan combine the butter andunsweetened chocolate. Cook over low heat, stirring constantly until smooth and well blended. Remove from heat and set aside.

In a large bowl, beat eggs, sugar and vanilla until thick and pale. Stir in the chocolate mixture and coffee liqueur. Fold in the flour. Stir in chopped walnuts if desired. Spread evenly into the prepared pan.

Bake for 30 to 35 minutes, or until a toothpick inserted in the center comes out almost clean. Be careful not to overbake. Cool for at least 30 minutes before cutting into bars and serving.

Peach Coffee Cake

Ingredients

- 1 (29 ounce) can sliced peaches, drained and chopped
- 1/4 cup brown sugar
- 1/2 tablespoon cornstarch
- 3 tablespoons vegetable oil
- 1 1/2 cups all-purpose flour
- 1 cup white sugar
- 1 tablespoon baking powder
- 2 lemons, zested
- 2 eggs, lightly beaten
- 1 teaspoon vanilla extract 1/2 cup vegetable oil
- 1/2 cup orange juice

Directions

Preheat oven to 350 degrees F (175 degrees C). Lightly grease an 8x8 inch baking pan.

In a saucepan over low heat, mix the peaches, brown sugar, cornstarch, and 3 tablespoons vegetable oil. Cook and stir until sugar is melted and mixture is slightly thickened.

In a large bowl, mix the flour, sugar, baking powder, and lemon zest. Stir in eggs, vanilla, 1/2 cup oil, and orange juice. Mix until smooth. Pour 1/2 the batter into the prepared pan. Layer with 1/2 the peach mixture, then with remaining batter. Top with remaining peach mixture.

Bake 45 minutes in the preheated oven, or until a knife inserted in the center comes out clean.

Cream Cheese Coffee Cakes

Ingredients

- 1/2 cup butter or margarine
- 1 cup sour cream
- 1/2 cup sugar
- 1 teaspoon salt
- 2 (.25 ounce) packages active dry yeast
- 1/2 cup warm water (110 degrees F to 115 degrees F)
- 2 eggs, lightly beaten
- 5 cups all-purpose flour
  CREAM CHEESE FILLING:
- 11 ounces cream cheese, softened
- 1/2 cup sugar 1 egg
- 1 1/2 teaspoons vanilla extract 1/4 teaspoon salt
- GLAZE:
- 2 cups confectioners' sugar 1/4 cup milk
- 2 teaspoons vanilla extract

Directions

In a saucepan, melt butter over low heat. Remove from the heat. Stir in sour cream, sugar and salt; cool to 110 degrees F-115 degrees F. In a mixing bowl, dissolve yeast in warm water.

Add the eggs, sour cream mixture and 2 cups flour; beat until smooth. Stir in enough remaining flour to form a stiff dough. Turn onto a floured surface; knead until smooth and elastic, about 6-8 minutes.

Place in a greased bowl, turning once to grease top. Cover and let rise in a warm place until doubled, about 1 hour.

In a mixing bowl, beat filling ingredients until smooth; set aside. Punch dough down. Turn onto a lightly floured surface; divide into four portions. Roll each into a 12-in. x 10-in. rectangle; spread with filling.

Roll up jelly-roll style, starting with a long side; pinch seam to seal and tuck ends under. Place seam side down on greased baking sheets. With a scissors, cut two-thirds of the way through dough at 1-in. intervals.

Cover and let rise until doubled, about 45 minutes.Bake at 350 degrees F for 15-20 minutes or until golden brown. Remove from pans to wire racks to cool. Combine glaze ingredients; drizzle over coffee cakes.

Coffee Liqueur Bread Pudding with Caramel

Ingredients

- 8 ounces cubed day old French bread
- 4 tablespoons butter, melted 1/2 cup chopped pecans
- 3 eggs
- 3/4 cup white sugar
- 4 teaspoons vanilla extract
- 1/2 teaspoon almond extract
- 1 pinch salt
- 3 cups milk
- 1 cup coffee flavored liqueur
- 1 teaspoon ground cinnamon
- 1 cup packed light brown sugar 1/2 cup butter
- 2 tablespoons light corn syrup

Directions

Preheat oven to 350 degrees F (175 degrees C). Grease a 1 1/2 quart shallow baking dish.

Set aside. Toss bread cubes with melted butter, and place half of them in prepared baking dish. Sprinkle with cherries or pecans. Top with remaining buttered bread cubes.In a large bowl, whisk eggs, 1/2 cup sugar, vanilla, almond extract and salt.

Heat milk and coffee liqueur in a small saucepan, then whisk into egg mixture. Pour mixture over bread. Press gently, tomoisten the bread cubes.

Let stand 30 minutes. Press bread cubes down again. Combine remaining 1/4 cup sugar and cinnamon in a bowl. Sprinkle mixture over pudding.To make the Caramel Sauce: In a 2 quart saucepan, bring brown sugar, butter, and corn syrup to a boil. Stir until smooth.

Boil for 1 minute. Pour over moistened bread cubes.Place baking dish in a larger baking pan. Pour some boiling water in the large pan halfway up the side of the smaller baking dish.

Bake for 45 to 50 minutes, or until golden. Serve warm.

Bread Machine Swedish Coffee Bread

Ingredients

- 1 cup milk
- 1/2 teaspoon salt
- 1 egg yolk
- 2 tablespoons softened butter
- 3 cups all-purpose flour 1/3 cup sugar
- 1 (.25 ounce) envelope active dry yeast
- 3 teaspoons ground cardamom
- 2 egg whites, slightly beaten pearl sugar, or other decorative sugar

Directions

Place ingredients in the pan of the bread machine in the order recommended by the manufacturer. Select dough cycle; press Start.

When the dough cycle has finished, divide into three equal portions. Roll each piece into a rope 12 to 14 inches long. Lay the three ropes side by side, then braid together. Tuck the ends underneath, and place onto a greased baking sheet, cover loosely with a towel, and allow to rise until doubled in bulk.

Preheat oven to 375 degrees F (190 degrees C).

Brush the braid with beaten egg white and sprinkle with pearl sugar. Bake in preheated oven until golden brown, 20 to 25 minutes.

Walnut-Rippled Coffee Cake

Ingredients

- 1 (18.25 ounce) package yellow cake mix
- 2 tablespoons sugar
- 4 eggs
- 1 cup sour cream 1/3 cup vegetable oil 1/4 cup water
- 1 cup chopped walnuts
- 2 tablespoons brown sugar
- 2 teaspoons ground cinnamon

Directions

Set aside 2 tablespoons cake mix. Place the remaining cake mix in a mixing bowl. Add sugar, eggs, sour cream, oil and water; beat on low speed for 2 minutes.

Pour half into a greased fluted 10-in. tube pan. Combine the walnuts, brown sugar, cinnamon and reserved cake mix; sprinkle over batter. Top with the remaining batter.

Bake at 350 degrees F for 40-45 minutes or until a toothpick inserted near the center comes out clean.

Cool for 10 minutes before removing from pan to a wire rack.

Dairy Free Cinnamon Streusel Coffee Cake

Ingredients

- 1/3 cup dairy free pancake mix (such as BisquickB®)
- 1/3 cup packed brown sugar
- 1/2 teaspoon ground cinnamon
- 3 tablespoons unsalted margarine
- 2 cups dairy free pancake mix (such as BisquickB®)
- 2/3 cup soy milk
- 2 tablespoons white sugar
- 1 egg, lightly beaten

Directions

Preheat oven to 375 degrees F (190 degrees C). Grease an 8-inch square baking pan and set aside. To make the streusel, combine 1/3 cup pancake mix, brown sugar, and cinnamon in a mixing bowl. Cut it the margarine until mixture is crumbly. (This can also be done in the food processor: pulse mixture 2 to 3 times to combine.)

Stir together the 2 cups of pancake mix, soy milk, sugar, and egg just until combined. Spread into prepared pan. Sprinkle with cinnamon streusel. Bake in preheated oven for 20 to 25 minutes, or until a toothpick inserted into the center of the cake comes out clean.

Cool before serving.

Kate Smith Coffee Cake

Ingredients

- 1 egg
- 1/4 cup butter or margarine, melted
- 1/3 cup milk
- 1 cup all-purpose flour 1/4 cup sugar
- 2 teaspoons baking powder 1/4 teaspoon salt
- 1 cup crushed bran flakes cereal TOPPING:
- 2 teaspoons butter or margarine, softened
- 2 tablespoons brown sugar
  1/3 cup bran flakes, crushed

Directions

In a mixing bowl, combine egg, butter and milk. Combine flour, sugar, baking powder and salt; stir into batter. Add bran flakes. Spread into a greased 8-in. round baking pan.
Combine topping ingredients; sprinkle over batter.

Bake at 375 degrees F for 18-22 minutes or until cake tests done.
Serve warm.

Chocolate Coffee Kiss

Ingredients

- 3/4 fluid ounce coffee liqueur
- 3/4 fluid ounce Irish cream liqueur
- 1/2 fluid ounce creme de cacao liqueur
- 1 teaspoon brandy-based orange liqueur (such as Grand Marnier®)
- 1 cup hot brewed coffee
- 2 tablespoons whipped cream
- 1 1/2 fluid ounces chocolate syrup
- 1 maraschino cherry

Directions

In a coffee mug, combine coffee liqueur, Irish cream, creme de cacao and Grand Marnier. Fill mug with hot coffee.

Top with a dollop of whipped cream, drizzle with chocolate syrup and garnish with a maraschino cherry.

Kahlua Irish Coffee

Ingredients

- 1 fluid ounce Kahlua
- 1 fluid ounce Jameson Irish Whiskey
- 3/4 cup hot coffee Whipped cream

Directions

Pour the Kahlua and Jameson Irish whiskey into a mug of hot coffee, top with whipped cream.

Eggnog Coffee Punch

Ingredients

- 1 1/2 cups coffee ice cream
- 1 1/2 cups eggnog
- 1 cup hot strongly brewed coffee
- 4 tablespoons frozen whipped topping, thawed
- 4 pinches ground nutmeg

Directions

Scoop the ice cream into a pan over low heat. Stir in the eggnog and coffee; and heat until warm, about 3 minutes.
Pour into four glass or ceramic mugs.

Top each with 1 tablespoon whipped topping and sprinkle with nutmeg. Serve immediately.

Cherry Lattice Coffee Cake

Ingredients

- 1 (.25 ounce) package active dry yeast
- 1/4 cup warm water (105 degrees to 115 degrees)
- 1 cup sour cream 1 egg
- 3 tablespoons sugar
- 2 tablespoons butter or margarine, softened
- 1 teaspoon salt
- 3 cups all-purpose flour FILLING:
- 2 1/2 cups fresh or frozen pitted tart cherries, thawed, rinsed and drained
- 1/2 cup sugar
- 1/2 cup chopped almonds, toasted
- 2 tablespoons all-purpose flour Dash salt

Directions

In a mixing bowl, dissolve yeast in water; let stand for 5 minutes. Add sour cream, egg, sugar, butter, salt and 2 cups flour; beat until smooth. Add enough remaining flour to form a soft dough.

Turn onto a floured surface; knead until smooth and elastic, abut 6-8 minutes. Place in a greased bowl, turning once to grease top.
Cover and let rise in a warm place until doubled, about 1 hour. Punch dough down.

Reserve 1 cup dough. Divide remaining dough in half. Roll each portion into a 9-in. circle; place in greased 9-in. round baking pans.

Combine filling ingredients; spread over dough to within 1/2 in. of edge. Roll out reserved dough to 1/4-in. thickness;

cut into 1/2-in. strips. Make a lattice top over filling. Cover and let rise until doubled, about 45 minutes. Bake at 375 degrees F for 15 minutes.

Cover top with foil; bake 20 minutes longer or until browned.

Streusel Coffee Cake Mix

Ingredients

- COFFEE CAKE MIX:
- 4 1/2 cups all-purpose flour
- 2 1/4 cups sugar
- 2 tablespoons baking powder
- 1 1/2 teaspoons salt
- STREUSEL MIX:
- 3/4 cup packed brown sugar
- 3 tablespoons all-purpose flour
- 1 tablespoon ground cinnamon 1/4 teaspoon ground nutmeg
- 1 1/2 cups chopped pecans
  ADDITIONAL INGREDIENTS:
- 1 egg, beaten
- 1/2 cup milk
- 1/4 cup vegetable oil
- 1 tablespoon butter or margarine, melted

Directions

Combine the cake mix ingredients; set aside. Combine the first four streusel ingredients; add pecans.

Store both mixes in separate airtight containers in a cool dry place for up to 6 months.

Jewish Coffee Cake I

Ingredients

- 2 1/2 cups all-purpose flour
- 1 1/4 teaspoons baking powder
- 1 1/4 teaspoons baking soda 3/4 cup butter, softened
- 1 1/4 cups white sugar
- 3 eggs
- 1 teaspoon vanilla extract
- 1 1/4 cups sour cream
- 1/4 cup butter, softened 1/2 cup all-purpose flour 1/4 cup white sugar
- 1 teaspoon ground cinnamon

Directions

Preheat an oven to 350 degrees F (175 degrees C).
Grease and flour a 9x13-inch baking dish. Combine 2 1/2 cups of flour, bakingpowder, and baking soda in a bowl. Beat the 3/4 cup of butter and 1 1/4 cups of sugar with an electric mixer in a large bowl until light and fluffy.

The mixture should benoticeably lighter in color. Add the room-temperature eggs one at a time, allowing each egg toblend into the butter mixture beforeadding the next. Beat in the vanilla with the last egg.

Pour in the flour mixture alternately with the sour cream, mixing until just incorporated. Batter will be thick. Pour the batter into prepared pan.

Mix 1/4 cup of butter, 1/2 cup of flour, 1/4 cup of sugar, and cinnamon in a small bowl until it resembles a coarse crumble. Sprinkle over the cake batter.

Bake in the preheated oven until a toothpick inserted into the center comes out clean, 30 to 35 minutes.

Cool in the pans for 10 minutes before removing to cool completely on a wire rack.

Sour Cream Coffee Cake

Ingredients

- 1/2 cup butter, softened
- 1 cup sugar
- 2 eggs
- 1 cup sour cream
- 1 teaspoon vanilla extract
- 2 cups all-purpose flour
- 1 teaspoon baking powder
- 1 teaspoon baking soda 1/4 teaspoon salt
- TOPPING:
  1/4 cup sugar
- 1/3 cup packed brown sugar
- 2 teaspoons ground cinnamon 1/2 cup chopped pecans

Directions

In a mixing bowl, cream butter and sugar.
Add eggs, sour cream and vanilla; mix well. Combine flour, baking powder, baking soda and salt; add to creamed mixture and beat until combined.

Pour half the batter into a greased 13-in. x 9-in. baking pan. Combine topping ingredients; sprinkle half of topping over batter.
Add remaining batter and topping. Bake at 325 degrees F for 40 minutes or until done.

Herman Coffee Cake

Ingredients

- 2 cups Herman Sourdough Starter 2/3 cup vegetable oil
- 2 eggs
- 2 cups all-purpose flour
- 1 1/2 teaspoons ground cinnamon 1/2 teaspoon baking soda
- 2 teaspoons baking powder 1/2 teaspoon salt
- 1 cup white sugar
- 1 cup chopped pecans
- 1 cup raisins
- 1 cup packed brown sugar
- 3 tablespoons all-purpose flour
- 1 teaspoon ground cinnamon 1/4 cup margarine, softened 1/2 cup margarine
- 1/4 cup milk
- 1 cup packed brown sugar

Directions

Bring Herman Starter to room temperature.

Preheat oven to 350 degrees F (175 degrees C). Grease and lightly flour one 9x13 inch baking pan. Stir together Herman Starter, oil and beaten eggs.

Stir together the flour, cinnamon, baking soda, baking powder, salt and white sugar. Stir in nuts and raisins. Add the flour mixture to the egg mixture and stir well.

Pour into the prepared pan and sprinkle with the topping. To Make Topping: Combine the 1 cup brown sugar, 3 tablespoons flour, 1 teaspoon cinnamon. Cut in 1/4 cup softened butter, until the mixture resembles very coarse crumbs.

Bake in a preheated 350 degrees F (175 degrees C) for 30 to 40 minutes. While still hot pour glaze over the top and serve.

To Make Glaze: In a small saucepan, melt 1/2 cup butter or margarine. Stir in the milk and 1 cup brown sugar.

Bring to a boil and let boil for 3 minutes. Immediately pour over hot cake.

Coffee Cookies

Ingredients

- 1/2 cup shortening 1 egg
- 2 tablespoons instant coffee powder
- 2/3 cup white sugar
- 1/2 cup chopped walnuts
- 1/2 teaspoon vanilla extract
- 3/4 cup all-purpose flour

Directions

Preheat oven to 350 degrees F (175 degrees C). Grease cookie sheets.

In a medium bowl, cream together the shortening, sugar and coffee. Beat in the egg, flour, vanilla and chopped nuts.

Mix until well
blended. Drop by teaspoonfuls onto cookie sheets

Bake for 10 to 12 minutes in the preheated oven, or until edges are golden. Let cool on wire racks.

Cranberry Coffee Cake

Ingredients

- 2 cups biscuit/baking mix
- 2 tablespoons sugar 2/3 cup milk
- 1 egg, beaten
- 2/3 cup jellied cranberry sauce TOPPING:
- 1/2 cup chopped walnuts
- 1/2 cup packed brown sugar
- 1/2 teaspoon ground cinnamon
  GLAZE:
- 1 cup confectioners' sugar
- 2 tablespoons milk
- 1/4 teaspoon vanilla extract

Directions

In a large bowl, combine the biscuit mix, sugar, milk and egg. Pour into a greased 8-in. square baking dish. Drop cranberry sauce by teaspoonfuls over batter.

Combine topping ingredients; sprinkle over cranberry sauce. Bake at 400 degrees F for 18-23 minutes or until a toothpick inserted near the center comes out clean. Cool on a wire rack.

In a small bowl, combine the glaze ingredients; drizzle over coffee cake.

Easy Iced Coffee

Ingredients

- 2 teaspoons instant coffee granules
- 1 teaspoon sugar
- 3 tablespoons warm water
- 6 fluid ounces cold milk

Directions

In sealable jar, combine instant coffee, sugar and warm water. Cover the jar and shake until it is foamy.

Pour into a glass full of ice. Fill the glass with milk. Adjust to taste if necessary.

Coffee Marinated Steak

Ingredients

- 2 tablespoons sesame seeds
- 6 tablespoons butter or margarine
- 1 medium onion, chopped
- 4 garlic cloves, minced
- 1 cup strong brewed coffee
- 1 cup soy sauce
- 2 tablespoons white vinegar
- 2 tablespoons Worcestershire sauce
- 2 pounds boneless beef top sirloin steak, cut 1 inch thick

Directions

In a skillet, toast sesame seeds in butter. Add onion and garlic; saute until tender. In a bowl, combine the coffee, soy sauce, vinegar, Worcestershire sauce and sesame seed mixture. Pour half into a large resealable plastic bag; add steak. Seal bag and turn to coat; refrigerate for 8 hours or overnight, turning occasionally.Cover and refrigerate remaining marinade.

Drain and discard marinade from steak. Grill steak, covered, over medium-hot heat for 6-10 minutes on each side or until meatreaches desired doneness (for medium-rare, a meat thermometer should read 145 degrees F; medium, 160 degrees F; well-done, 170 degrees F). Warm reserved marinade and serve with steak.

Cheese-Filled Coffee Cakes

Ingredients

- 2 (.25 ounce) packages active dry yeast
- 1/2 cup warm water (110 degrees F to 115 degrees F)
- 1 cup sour cream
- 1/2 cup butter or margarine 1/2 cup sugar
- 1 teaspoon salt
- 2 eggs
- 4 1/2 cups all-purpose flour FILLING:
- 2 (8 ounce) packages cream cheese, softened
- 3/4 cup sugar 1 egg
- 1 teaspoon almond extract 1/8 teaspoon salt
- GLAZE:
- 2 cups confectioners' sugar
- 3 tablespoons milk
- 1/2 teaspoon vanilla extract

Directions

In a mixing bowl, dissolve yeast in warm water. In a saucepan, heat sour cream and butter to 110 degrees F-115 degrees F. Add the sour cream mixture, sugar, salt and eggs to yeast mixture; mix well.

Gradually add flour; mix well. Do not knead. Cover and refrigerate for 2 hours.

In a mixing bowl, beat filling ingredients until smooth. Set aside. Turn doug onto a lightly floured surface; divide into four pieces. Roll each into a 12-in. x 8-in. rectangle.

Spread filling to within ½ in. of edges. Roll up, jelly-roll style, starting with a long side; pinch seam to seal and tuck ends under.

Place, seam side down, on two greased baking sheets. With a sharp knife, make deep slashes across the top of each loaf

Cover and let rise in a warm place until doubled, about 1 hour. Bake at 375 degrees F for 20-25 minutes or until golden brown.

Remove from pans to wire racks. Combine glaze ingredients; drizzle over warm loaves. Cool. Refrigerate

Pralines, Coffee and Cream Cake

Ingredients

- 1 (18.25 ounce) package white cake mix
- 3 eggs
- 1 cup coffee flavored liqueur 1/2 cup vegetable oil
- 1 cup butter
- 1 cup packed brown sugar
- 1 1/2 cups chopped pecans
- 1 (3.5 ounce) package instant vanilla pudding mix
- 1 1/2 cups milk
- 8 ounces cream cheese
- 1 (12 ounce) container frozen whipped topping, thawed

Directions

Preheat oven to 350 degrees F (175 degrees C). Lightly grease and flour one 9x13 inch pan. Combine cake mix, eggs, coffee liqueur and oil in large bowl and mix on medium speed for approximately 2 minutes. Pour into prepared pan.

Bake at 350 degrees F (175 degrees C) for approximately 25 minutes (may vary). Done when cake springs back to the touch or toothpick inserted in center comes out clean. Set aside on cooling rack. To make pralines: combine butter and brown sugar in small saucepan. Heat on medium to medium high, stirring constantly. Bring to boil for 2 minutes, again stirring constantly. Pour in pecans and remove from heat. Stir, then immediately pour pralines over cake. Cool cake in refrigerator. To make frosting: combine pudding mix, milk, cream cheese, and nondairy whipped topping, and beat with electric mixer until well mixed. Spread on cake. Ready to serve!

Tropical Coffee Cake

Ingredients

- 1 cup sugar
- 1/2 cup vegetable oil
- 2 eggs
- 1 cup sour cream
- 1 1/2 cups all-purpose flour
- 2 teaspoons baking powder 1/2 teaspoon salt
- 1 (8 ounce) can crushed pineapple, drained
- TOPPING:
- 1/2 cup flaked coconut
- 3 tablespoons sugar
  1/2 teaspoon ground cinnamon

Directions

In a mixing bowl, blend the sugar and oil. Add eggs, one at a time, beating well after each addition. Beat in sour cream. Combine the flour, baking powder and salt; add to the sour cream mixture. Stir in pineapple.

Transfer to a greased 9-in. square baking dish. Combine the topping ingredients; sprinkle over batter. Bake at 350 degrees F for 35-40 minutes or until a toothpick inserted near the center comes out clean. Cool on a wire rack.

Pumpkin Coffee Ring

Ingredients

- 2 1/4 cups all-purpose flour 3/4 cup sugar, divided
- 1 (.25 ounce) package active dry yeast
- 1/2 teaspoon salt 1/4 cup water
- 1/4 cup milk
- 3 tablespoons butter or margarine 1 egg
- 1 (3 ounce) package cream cheese, softened
- 1/2 cup canned or cooked pumpkin
- 1 teaspoon ground cinnamon 1/2 teaspoon salt
- 1/2 teaspoon ground ginger 1/2 teaspoon ground nutmeg 1/2 cup chopped walnuts
- 1/2 cup raisins
- 1 egg yolk, beaten GLAZE:
- 1/2 cup confectioners' sugar   1/8 teaspoon vanilla extract
- 1 tablespoon milk
- 1/4 cup finely chopped walnuts

Directions

In a mixing bowl, combine 1-1/2 cups flour, 1/4 cup sugar, yeast and salt. In a saucepan, heat water, milk and butter to 120 degrees F-130 degrees F.
Add to dry ingredients; beat just until moistened.

Beat in egg. Stir in enough remaining flour to form a soft dough.
Turn onto a floured surface; knead until smooth and elastic, about 6-8 minutes. Place in a greased bowl, turning once to grease top. Cover and let rise in a warm place until doubled, about 1 hour.

In a small mixing bowl, beat cream cheese and remaining sugar until smooth. Add the pumpkin, cinnamon, salt, ginger and nutmeg. Punch dough down; turn onto a floured surface. Roll into a 20-in x 10-in. rectangle; spread pumpkin mixture to within 1/2 in. of edges.

Sprinkle with nuts and raisins. Roll up jelly-roll style, starting with a long side; pinch ends together to form a ring. Place on a greased baking sheet. Cover and let rise until doubled, about 1 hour.
Brush dough with egg yolk. Bake at 350 degrees F for 20-25 minutes or until golden brown.

Remove from pan to a wire rack. For glaze, combine the confectioners' sugar, vanilla and enough milk to achieve drizzling consistency.
Drizzle over warm ring. Sprinkle with nuts.

Herman Coffee Cake

Ingredients

- 1 cup sourdough starter
- 1 cup white sugar
- 2 cups self-rising flour 1/2 teaspoon salt
- 2 teaspoons ground cinnamon 2/3 cup vegetable oil
- 2 eggs
- 1 cup raisins or dates
- 1 cup chopped walnuts
- 1 tablespoon honey (optional)
- 1 cup packed brown sugar
- 1 teaspoon all-purpose flour
- 1 teaspoon ground cinnamon 1/4 cup chopped walnuts
- 1/2 cup butter
- 1 cup sifted confectioners' sugar
- 2 tablespoons butter, melted
- 2 tablespoons milk

Directions

To Make Starter: Mix 2 cups flour, 1/4 cup sugar, 2 cups warm water, 1/4 ounce yeast in a bowl, cover and let stand over night (cover should be loose).

Refrigerate and stir daily. On fifth day feed Herman one cup flour, 1 cup milk and 1/2 cup sugar; stir and refrigerate.
Stir daily until 10th day. On 10th day remove 1 cup starter and feed as on fifth day.Preheat oven to 350 degrees F (175 degrees C).

Grease four 8 inch pans or three 9 inch pans. Mix together 1 cup starter, white sugar, self rising flour, salt, 2 teaspoons cinnamon, oil, eggs, raisins, 1 cup chopped nuts, honey (optional). Stir until combined. Pour into prepared pans. Top with sugar-nut topping.

Dot with 1/2 cup butter or margarine and bake at 350 degrees F (175 degrees C) for 15 minutes.

Remove cakes from oven and pour glaze over still-warm cakes.
To Make Sugar-Nut Topping: Mix together 1 cup brown sugar, 1 teaspoon flour, 1 teaspoon cinnamon, 1/4 cup chopped nuts.
To Make Glaze: Combine 1 cup sifted confectioners' sugar, 2 tablespoons melted margarine, 2 tablespoons milk.

Use immediately to glaze cake.

Cherry Almond Coffeecake

Ingredients

- 1 cup sour cream 1/4 cup water
- 3 eggs
- 1 (18.25 ounce) package white cake mix
- 1 (21 ounce) can cherry pie filling 1/4 cup sliced almonds
- 1 1/2 cups confectioners' sugar
- 2 tablespoons milk
- 1 dash vegetable oil

Directions

Preheat oven to 350 degrees F (175 degrees C). Generously grease and flour one 15 1/2x 10 1/2 inch jelly roll pan.

Mix sour cream, water and eggs. Stir in cake mix until moistened. You will notice the batter will be lumpy. Spread into pan. Drop pie filling by large spoonfuls onto batter.

Bake at 350 degrees F (175 degrees C) for 25 minutes or until cake tests done. Sprinkle cake with almonds and drizzle with glaze.

To Make Glaze: Mix confectioner's sugar, milk and vegetable oil. Stir in a few extra drops of milk if necessary. Stir until mixture is smooth and of a desired consistency. Drizzle over still warm cake.

Coffee Bonbons

Ingredients

- 1 cup butter
- 3/4 cup confectioners' sugar
- 1/2 teaspoon vanilla extract
- 1 tablespoon instant coffee granules
- 1 3/4 cups all-purpose flour CHOCOLATE GLAZE:
- 1 tablespoon butter
- 1/2 ounce unsweetened chocolate
- 1 cup confectioners' sugar
- 2 tablespoons milk

Directions

In a mixing bowl, cream butter and sugar until light and fluffy.
Add vanilla. Combine coffee and flour; stir into creamed mixture and mix well. Chill. Shape into 3/4-in. balls and place on ungreased baking sheets. Bake at 350 degrees F for 18-20 minutes.

Meanwhile, for glaze, melt butter and chocolate together. Add melted mixture to sugar along with milk; beat until smooth. Frost cookies while still warm.

Almond Coffee Creamer

Ingredients

- 3/4 cup confectioners' sugar 3/4 cup powdered non-dairy creamer
- 1 teaspoon ground cinnamon
- 1 teaspoon almond extract

Directions

In a bowl, combine all the ingredients; mix well. Store in an airtight container.

To use, add to coffee in place of nondairy creamer and sugar.

Coffee Nudge

Ingredients

- 8 cups hot brewed coffee
- 8 fluid ounces coffee flavored liqueur
- 8 fluid ounces brandy
- 4 fluid ounces creme de cacao
- 2 cups whipped cream, garnish
- 2 tablespoons chocolate sprinkles

Directions

In the bottom of 8 coffee mugs, pour 1 ounce each coffee liqueur and brandy. Pour in 1/2 ounce each creme de cacao.

Fill each cup with hot coffee and garnish with a dollop of whipped cream and chocolate sprinkles.

Coffeebar Chai

Ingredients

- 2 cups water
- 4 black tea bags 1/4 cup honey
- 1/2 teaspoon vanilla extract
- 1 cinnamon stick
- 5 whole cloves
- 1/4 teaspoon ground cardamom 1/4 teaspoon ground ginger
- 1 pinch ground nutmeg
- 2 cups milk

Directions

In a saucepan, bring water to a boil. Add tea, honey and vanilla. Season with cinnamon, cloves, cardamom, ginger and nutmeg. Simmer for 5 minutes. Pour in milk, and bring to a boil.

Remove from heat, and strain through a fine sieve.

Cherry Swirl Coffee Cake

Ingredients

- 1 1/2 cups sugar
- 1/2 cup butter or margarine 1/2 cup shortening
- 1/2 teaspoon baking powder
- 1 teaspoon vanilla extract
- 1 teaspoon almond extract
- 4 eggs
- 3 cups all-purpose flour
- 1 (21 ounce) can cherry pie filling GLAZE:
- 1 cup confectioners' sugar
- 1 tablespoon milk

Directions

In a mixing bowl, blend the first seven ingredients on low speed. Increase to high speed and whip for 3 minutes. Stir in flour.

Spread 2/3 of the batter over the bottom of a greased 15-1/2-in. x 10-1/2-in. x 1-in. jelly roll pan.

Spread pie filling over batter; drop remaining batter by tablespoonsful over all. Bake at 350 degrees F for 40 minutes or until golden.

Meanwhile, combine glaze ingredients. Drizzle over cake while warm. Cake is best if served immediately.

Banana Coffee Cake

Ingredients

- 1 (8 ounce) package cream cheese, softened
- 1/2 cup butter or margarine, softened
- 1 1/4 cups sugar
- 2 eggs
- 1 cup mashed ripe bananas
- 1 teaspoon vanilla extract
- 2 1/4 cups all-purpose flour
- 1 1/2 teaspoons baking powder 1/2 teaspoon baking soda
- TOPPING:
- 1 cup chopped pecans
- 2 tablespoons sugar
- 1 teaspoon ground cinnamon

Directions

In a mixing bowl, beat the cream cheese, butter and sugar. Add eggs, one at a time, beating well after each addition. Add the bananas and vanilla.

Combine flour, baking powder and baking soda; gradually add to the creamed mixture.

Combine topping ingredients; add half to batter. Transfer to a greased 13-in. x 9-in. x 2-in. baking pan. Sprinkle with the remaining topping.
Bake at 350 degrees F for 25-30 minutes or until a toothpick inserted near the center comes out clean. Cool on a wire rack.

Royal Rhubarb Coffee Cake

Ingredients

- 1/3 cup butter, softened
- 1 cup sugar
- 1 egg
- 1 teaspoon vanilla extract
- 2 cups all-purpose flour
- 3 teaspoons baking powder 1/2 teaspoon salt
- 1 cup milk
- 2 1/2 cups diced fresh or frozen rhubarb, thawed
- TOPPING:
- 3/4 cup packed brown sugar 1/4 cup butter, melted
- 1 teaspoon ground cinnamon

Directions

In a large mixing bowl, cream butter and sugar until light and fluffy. Add egg and vanilla; beat well. Combine the flour, baking powder and salt; add to creamed mixture alternately with milk

Transfer to a greased 13-in. x 9-in. x 2-in. baking dish. Spoon rhubarb over top to within 1/2 in. of edges. Combine topping ingredients; sprinkle over rhubarb.

Bake at 350 degrees F for 45-55 minutes or until a toothpick inserted near the center comes out clean. Cool in pan on a wire rack.

Candy Cane Coffee Cake

Ingredients

- 1 tablespoon active dry yeast 1/4 cup warm water (105 degrees to 115 degrees)
- 1/2 cup butter or margarine, softened
- 1/2 cup sour cream
- 2 eggs
- 3 tablespoons sugar 1/4 teaspoon salt
- 3 cups all-purpose flour FILLING:
- 2 (8 ounce) packages cream cheese, softened
- 1/2 cup sugar
- 2 egg yolks
- 2 teaspoons vanilla extract TOPPINGS:
- 1 tablespoon confectioners' sugar
- 1 (12 ounce) jar cherry jam

Directions

In a small bowl, dissolve yeast in warm water. In a mixing bowl, combine the butter, sour cream, eggs, sugar and salt. Add yeast mixture and flour; beat until smooth (do not knead).

Place in a greased bowl, turning once to grease top. Cover and refrigerate overnight.

For filling, in a mixing bowl, beat cream cheese, sugar, egg yolk and vanilla until blended. Punch dough down. Turn onto a lightly floured surface; divided in half. Roll out each portion into a 16-in. x 10-in. rectangle on a greased baking sheet.

Spread filling down center of each rectangle. On each long side, cut 1-1/2-in.-wide strips about 3 in. into center. Starting at one end, fold alternating strips at an angle across filling. Pinch ends to seal.

Curve one end, forming a candy cane. Cover and let rise until doubled, about 1 hour.

Bake at 350 degrees F for 20-25 minutes or until golden brown. Carefully remove from pans to wire racks to cool. Sprinkle with confectioners' sugar. Stir jam, then spoon over top of leaves, creating candy cane stripes.

Refrigerate leftovers.

Chocolate Chip Coffee Cake

Ingredients

- 1 cup butter or margarine, softened
- 1 (8 ounce) package cream cheese, softened
- 1 1/2 cups sugar, divided
- 2 eggs
- 1 teaspoon vanilla extract
- 2 cups all-purpose flour
- 1 teaspoon baking powder 1/2 teaspoon baking soda 1/4 teaspoon salt
- 1/4 cup milk
- 1 cup semisweet chocolate chips 1/4 cup chopped pecans
- 1 teaspoon ground cinnamon

Directions

In a mixing bowl, cream the butter, cream cheese and 1-1/4 cups of sugar. Beat in eggs and vanilla. Combine the flour, baking powder, baking soda and salt; add to creamed mixture alternately with milk. Stir in chocolate chips. Pour into a greased 9-in. springform pan. Combine the pecans, cinnamon and remaining sugar; sprinkle over batter.

Bake at 350 degrees F for 50-55 minutes or until a toothpick inserted near the center comes out clean. Cool for 15 minutes. Carefully run a knife around edge of pan to loosen.

Remove sides of pan. Cool completely before cutting.

Iced Coffee

Ingredients

- 1/2 cup warm water
- 2 teaspoons instant coffee granules
- 1 tray ice cubes
- 1/2 (5 ounce) can sweetened condensed milk, divided
- 1/2 cup milk
- 1 tablespoon chocolate syrup

Directions

In a small bowl, stir together the water and instant coffee.

In a blender, combine ice cubes, coffee mixture, milk, sweetened condensed milk and chocolate syrup.

Blend until smooth.

Pour into glasses and serve.

Coffee Whirl

Ingredients

- 1 scoop vanilla ice cream
- 2 tablespoons strong brewed coffee, cold
- 1/4 teaspoon unsweetened cocoa powder

Directions

In a blender, combine ice cream, coffee and cocoa. Blend until smooth. Pour into glasses and serve.

Buttermilk Coffee Cake

Ingredients

- 2 1/2 cups all-purpose flour
- 1 cup packed brown sugar 3/4 cup sugar
- 3/4 cup vegetable oil
- 1 teaspoon salt
- 1 egg, lightly beaten
- 1 cup buttermilk
- 1 teaspoon baking soda TOPPING:
- 1 cup chopped pecans
- 1/4 cup packed brown sugar 1/4 cup sugar
- 1 tablespoon all-purpose flour
- 3/4 teaspoon ground cinnamon
- 1/2 teaspoon ground nutmeg

Directions

In a mixing bowl, combine flour, sugars, oil and salt; mix well. Remove 1/2 cup and set aside.

To remaining flour mixture, add egg, buttermilk and baking soda; mix well. Pour into a greased 15-in. x 10-in. x 1-in. baking pan. To reserved flour mixture add all topping ingredients; mix well.

Sprinkle over batter. Bake at 350 degrees F for 25-30 minutes or until cake tests done.

Coffee Roasted Beef Chuck

Ingredients

- 2 tablespoons butter
- 1 tablespoon vegetable oil
- 4 pounds beef chuck roast
- 2 large yellow onions, chopped
- 2 cloves garlic, minced
- freshly ground pepper, to taste
- 6 cups brewed coffee
- 2 cups sliced fresh mushrooms
- 3 tablespoons cornstarch salt to taste
- 1/2 cup sour cream

Directions

In a large pot, heat the butter and oil over medium/high heat. Place the roast in the pot and sear it on all sides until well browned.

Remove the roast and set aside.

In the same pot, saute the onions for 5 minutes, scraping loose the brown roast bits on the bottom of the pot. Add the garlic and pepper and saute for 1 minute. Return the meat to the pot and pour in the coffee and add the mushrooms.

Over high heat, bring to a boil. Reduce heat to low and simmer for 5 hours, turning the meat over halfway through the cooking time. A slow cooker may be used for cooking the roast, if desired.

To make the gravy: When the roast is done, remove it from the pot. Take 1/2 cup of the coffee sauce mixture from the pot and stir in the cornstarch to make a slurry. Mix well. Return the slurry to the pot, stirring until the sauce thickens slightly. Stir in the sour cream then salt to taste.

66

Sara's Iced Coffee

Ingredients

- 4 cups fresh brewed coffee 1/2 teaspoon vanilla extract(optional)
- 1/4 cup white sugar
- 1/4 cup boiling water
- 3 cups crushed ice 1/2 cup cream

Directions

Refrigerate coffee until cool, about 30 minutes. Chill four glasses, if desired. Stir vanilla extract and sugar in the boiling water until dissolved. Refrigerate until cool, about 30 minutes.

Divide the ice and chilled coffee evenly between the four glasses. Stir in cream and sugar mixture, to taste.

Crispy Coffee Cookies

Ingredients

- 1 cup sugar
- 3/4 cup vegetable oil
- 1/3 cup instant coffee granules
- 2 tablespoons hot water
- 2 eggs
- 2 1/2 cups all-purpose flour
- 1 1/2 teaspoons baking powder 3/4 teaspoon salt
- Additional sugar

Directions

In a mixing bowl, combine sugar and oil. Dissolve coffee in water; add to sugar mixture and mix well. Add eggs, one at a time, beating well after each addition. Combine the flour, baking powder and salt; gradually add to the sugar mixture.

Roll into 3/4-in. balls, then roll in additional sugar. Place 2 in. apart on lightly greased baking sheets; flatten with a fork. Bake at 400 degrees F for 8-10 minutes or until edges are firm. Remove to wire racks to cool.

Overnight Coffee Cake

Ingredients

- 1/3 cup butter, softened 1/2 cup white sugar
- 1/4 cup packed brown sugar 1 egg
- 1 cup all-purpose flour
- 1/2 teaspoon baking powder 1/4 teaspoon baking soda
- 1/2 teaspoon ground cinnamon 1/2 cup buttermilk
- 1/4 cup packed brown sugar
- 1/4 cup finely chopped walnuts
- 1/4 teaspoon ground cinnamon

Directions

Lightly grease an 8 inch square baking pan. In a large bowl, cream together the butter, white sugar, and 1/4 cup brown sugar. Beat in the egg until well blended. In a medium bowl, combine the flour, baking powder, baking soda, and 1/2 teaspoon cinnamon. Stir the flour mixture into the creamed mixture alternately with buttermilk. Spread evenly into the prepared baking pan.

In a small bowl, mix 1/4 cup brown sugar, walnuts, and 1/4 teaspoon cinnamon. Sprinkle over the batter. Cover, and refrigerate overnight.

The next day, preheat oven to 350 degrees F (175 degrees C). Bake the cake for 40 to 45 minutes in the preheated oven, or until a toothpick inserted in the center comes out clean.

Lemon Blueberry Coffee Cake

Ingredients

- 1 egg, lightly beaten 1/3 cup sugar
- 1 teaspoon grated lemon peel 2/3 cup milk
- 2 1/4 cups biscuit baking mix
- 1 cup fresh or frozen blueberries* 3/4 cup confectioners' sugar
- 4 teaspoons lemon juice

Directions

In a bowl, combine the egg, sugar, lemon peel and milk; mix well. Stir in the biscuit mix just until moistened. Fold in blueberries. Pour into a greased 9-in. round baking pan.

Bake at 350 degrees F for 25-30 minutes or until a toothpick inserted near the center comes out clean. cool for 10 minutes before removing from pan to a wire rack.

Combine the confectioners' sugar and lemon juice until smooth; drizzle over warm cake. Cut into wedges.

Bran Muffins with Coffee

Ingredients

- 2 eggs
- 3/4 cup white sugar
- 1/3 cup butter, melted
- 1 cup brewed coffee
- 2 tablespoons buttermilk
- 2 1/2 cups all-purpose flour
- 2 1/2 teaspoons baking soda
- 3 cups whole bran cereal

Directions

In a large bowl, mix together the eggs, white sugar and butter until smooth. Stir in the buttermilk and coffee. The mixture will look curdled. Combine the flour and baking soda; stir into the coffee mixture. Blend in bran cereal. Cover and refrigerate for at least 20 minutes or up to a week.

Preheat the oven to 375 degrees F (190 degrees C). Grease a muffin pan or line with paper muffin liners. Fill each cup with 1/4 cup batter.

Bake for 18 to 20 minutes in the preheated oven, or until the top springs back when lightly touched. Cool in pan before removing.

Sugar Free Blueberry Coffee Cake

Ingredients

- 3/4 cup butter, melted and cooled
- 1 cup milk
- 3 eggs
- 1 teaspoon vanilla extract
- 1 1/2 cups granular sucrolose sweetener (such as Splenda®)
- 2 teaspoons baking powder
- 3 cups all-purpose flour
- 1 3/4 cups fresh or frozen blueberries
- 1 1/2 cups malitol brown sugar substitute
- 3/4 cup flour
- 2 teaspoons ground cinnamon 1/2 cup butter, softened

Directions

Preheat the oven to 350 degrees F (175 degrees C). Grease and flour a 9x13 inch baking pan.

In a large bowl, stir together the melted butter, milk, eggs, vanilla and 1 1/2 cups sugar substitute. Combine 3 cups of flour and baking powder; stir into the wet ingredients until just blended. Fold in the blueberries. Spread evenly in the prepared pan.

In a small bowl, stir together the brown sugar substitute, 3/4 cup of flour, and cinnamon. Stir in the softened butter with a fork until the mixture is crumbly. Sprinkle over the top of the cake.

Bake for 35 to 40 minutes in the preheated oven, until a toothpick inserted into the center of the cake comes out clean. This cake is best served warm.

Blueberry Coffee Cake

Ingredients

- Ingredients for Coffee Cake:
  Crisco® Flour No-Stick Cooking Spray
- 1 1/2 cups all-purpose flour, divided
- 1/4 cup sugar
- 2 1/2 teaspoons baking powder 1/2 teaspoon salt
- 1/4 teaspoon ground allspice
- 1/3 cup butter or margarine, melted
- 1 egg
- 2/3 cup milk
- 3/4 cup SMUCKER'S® Blueberry Preserves Ingredients for Topping:
- 1/4 cup firmly packed brown sugar
- 1/4 cup chopped walnuts
- 2 tablespoons flour
- 1 tablespoon butter or margarine

Directions

Heat oven to 400 degrees F. Spray 8- or 9-inch square baking pan with no-stick cooking spray. Lightly spoon flour into measuring cup; level off.

In medium bowl, combine 1 1/2 cups flour, sugar, baking powder, salt and allspice. Add melted butter, egg and milk. Mix vigorously until well blended.

Pour half of batter into greased and floured pan; spread SMUCKER'S® preserves evenly over batter. Top with remaining batter.

Combine topping ingredients; mix until crumbly. Sprinkle over top of coffee cake.

Bake at 400 degrees for 20 to 25 minutes or until toothpick inserted in center comes out clean.

Kahlua Coffee

Ingredients

- 2 fluid ounces Kahlua
- 3 fluid ounces coffee

Directions

Add Kahlua to coffee.

Garnish with orange peel or a cinnamon stick.

Hot Coffee Frosting

Ingredients

- 1 (16 ounce) package confectioners' sugar
- 3 tablespoons butter, softened
- 6 tablespoons unsweetened cocoa powder
- 1 teaspoon vanilla extract up hot,
- ¼ brewed coffee

Directions

In a large bowl, combine confectioners' sugar, butter, cocoa powder and vanilla. Beat on slow speed until ingredients are combined. While beating, slowly add hot coffee until desired consistency is achieved.

Coffee Jelly

Ingredients

- 1 (.25 ounce) package unflavored gelatin
- 2 tablespoons hot water
- 3 tablespoons white sugar
- 2 cups fresh brewed coffee

Directions

Dissolve gelatin in the hot water in a small bowl. Pour gelatin mixture, coffee, and sugar in a saucepan and bring to a boil over high heat. Pour coffee mixture into glasses for individual servings or a large pan for cubing. Chill in the refrigerator until solidified, 6 to 7 hours.

Old-Fashioned German Coffee Cake

Ingredients

- 2 (0.6 ounce) cakes compressed yeast cake, crumbled
- 1 tablespoon sugar
- 1/2 cup warm water (80 to 90 degrees F)
- 1/3 cup shortening, melted 1/2 cup sugar
- 1 egg, beaten
- 3 1/2 cups all-purpose flour, divided
- 1/2 cup warm milk (80 to 90 degrees F)
- TOPPING:
- 1 cup all-purpose flour
- 1/2 cup packed brown sugar 1/2 cup sugar
- 1/4 cup shortening
- 2 teaspoons vanilla extract Pinch salt
- 2 (16 ounce) cans peaches in heavy syrup, drained

Directions

Dissolve yeast and 1 tablespoon sugar in water; let stand 5 minutes. In a large mixing bowl, combine shortening, sugar and egg.

Gradually mix in 2 cups flour, milk and yeast mixture. Add enough remaining flour to form a soft dough. Turn out onto a floured surface; knead until smooth and elastic, about 6-8 minutes.

Place dough in a greased bowl, turning to grease top. Cover and let rise in a warm place until doubled, about 1 hour. Punch dough down. Divide in half; press each half into a greased 11-in. x 7-in. baking pan.

Cover and let rise until doubled, about 1 hour. For topping, combine flour, sugars, shortening, vanilla and salt; sprinkle over dough. Arrange peaches on top.

Bake at 375 degrees F for 25-30 minutes or until golden brown.

Streusel Apple Coffeecake

Ingredients

- 1 1/2 cups packed light brown sugar
- 3/4 cup all-purpose flour
- 1/2 cup butter, chilled and diced
- 2 teaspoons ground cinnamon
- 1 cup chopped walnuts
- 3 1/4 cups all-purpose flour
- 1 1/2 teaspoons baking powder 3/4 teaspoon baking soda
- 3/4 cup butter, room temperature
- 1 1/2 cups white sugar
- 3 eggs
- 2 teaspoons vanilla extract
- 16 ounces plain low-fat yogurt
- 2 Granny Smith apples - peeled, cored and finely diced

Directions

Preheat oven to 350 degrees F (175 degrees C). Grease and flour a Bundt cake pan. To make streusel: In a medium bowl, mix brown sugar, 3/4 cup flour, and cinnamon. Cut in the butter with a fork until crumbly. Stir in walnuts.

In a medium bowl, stir together 3 1/4 cups flour, baking powder, and baking soda. In a large bowl, cream together the butter and sugar until light and fluffy. Beat in the eggs one at a time, mixing well after each. Then stir in the vanilla and yogurt.

Gently stir in the flour mixture just until blended.

Pour 3 cups of the batter into the Bundt pan, sprinkle with 1/4 of the streusel, and layer with apples. Sprinkle with 1/2 the remaining streusel. Pour in the remaining batter, and top with the remaining 1/4 streusel.

Lightly pat the top layer of streusel so it sticks to the cake batter. Bake 50 to 60 minutes in the preheated oven, or until a toothpick inserted in the center comes out clean.

Cool in the pan on a wire rack 15 minutes. Place cookie sheet over pan and carefully invert both. Remove Bundt pan, and let the cake cool completely.

Smucker's® Cherry Swirl Coffee Cake

Ingredients

- 1 1/4 cups milk
- 1 teaspoon salt
- 1/4 cup granulated sugar
- 1/2 cup Crisco® All-Vegetable Shortening
- 1 (.25 ounce) package active dry yeast
- 3 1/4 cups Pillsbury BEST® All Purpose Flour
- 2 eggs
- 1/2 teaspoon vanilla
- 1 cup Smucker's® Cherry Preserves
- 1 cup powdered sugar Milk
- 1/3 cup sliced almonds

Directions

Heat 1-1/4 cups milk, salt, granulated sugar, and shortening in small saucepan just to boiling; cool to lukewarm (105 degrees F to 115 degrees F). Stir in yeast; transfer mixture to medium bowl.

Add one cup of the flour to milk mixture; beat well. Add eggs and vanilla; beat well. Stir in enough remaining flour to make a thick batter; beat until smooth. Let rise, covered, in warm place, free from drafts, until doubled in bulk, about one hour. Stir batter down.

Pour batter into two greased nine-inch round cake pans; let rise in warm place until doubled in bulk, about one hour. Make a swirl design on top of batter with a floured spoon; fillgrooves with preserves, using 1/4 cup for each coffee cake.Heat oven to 375 degrees F.

Bake coffee cakes until golden, 30 to 35 minutes. Remove from pans, cool on wire racks.

Fill grooves with remaining preserves.

Mix powdered sugar, with enough milk to make thin glaze consistency; drizzle over warm coffee cakes.

Sprinkle with almonds.

Coconut Coffee Liqueur Cake

Ingredients

- 1 (18.25 ounce) package yellow cake mix
- 2 1/2 teaspoons instant coffee granules
- 1/2 cup coffee flavored liqueur
- 2 cups milk
- 1 (5 ounce) package instant vanilla pudding mix
- 1 1/2 cups heavy whipping cream
- 3 tablespoons white sugar
- 3 cups flaked coconut

Directions

Add instant coffee to cake mix and prepare cake according to instructions on package. Pour batter into 2 greased and floured 9 inch cake pans. Bake according to instructions on package. Allow to cool.

With a large serrated knife, split each layer horizontally to make 4 layers. Sprinkle 1/4 cup of the coffee liqueur on each of the 4 layers.

Make the pudding according to package directions, but add the remaining 1/4 cup of coffee liqueur. Spread 1/3 of pudding between each layer of cake as you assemble. Whip cream with sugar until stiff peaks form. Spread on top and sides of cake.

Sprinkle with coconut.

Coffee and Donuts Ice Cream

Ingredients

- 4 marble crullers (fried twisted stick doughnuts)
- 1 cup milk
- 2 tablespoons instant coffee granules
- 2 eggs
- 3/4 cup white sugar
- 2 cups heavy cream

Directions

Crumble or chop the crullers into small pieces. Do not over chop into crumbs, but make a variety of piece sizes. Set the doughnut pieces aside.

Gently heat the milk in a saucepan over low heat until hot but not boiling, and stir in the instant coffee granules until dissolved. Remove the milk mixture from the heat, and allow to cool.

Place the eggs in a mixing bowl, and beat for 3 minutes with an electric mixer until light, adding sugar about 2 tablespoons at a time until the sugar has been incorporated. Beat for 1 more minute, then beat the milk mixture and heavy cream into the eggs on low speed, until the mixture is smooth and creamy.

Place the mixture into an ice cream maker, and freeze according to manufacturer's instructions. When the ice cream is firm but not hard, lightly mix in the doughnut pieces. Pack the ice cream into a covered airtight container, and freeze for 6 to 8 hours, to ripen the flavor and firm the ice cream. Let the ice cream stand at room temperature for about 10 minutes before scooping into servings.

Cranberry Banana Coffee Cake

Ingredients

- 1/2 cup butter or margarine, softened
- 1/2 cup sugar
- 2 eggs
- 1 teaspoon vanilla extract
- 2 cups all-purpose flour
- 2 teaspoons baking powder
- 1 teaspoon ground cinnamon 1/4 teaspoon salt
- 1/4 teaspoon ground allspice
- 2 medium ripe bananas, mashed
- 1 cup whole berry cranberry sauce
- TOPPING:
- 1/2 cup packed brown sugar 1/2 cup chopped pecans
- 2 tablespoons all-purpose flour
- 2 tablespoons butter or margarine, melted

Directions

In a large mixing bowl, cream the butter and sugar. Beat in eggs and vanilla. Combine the dry ingredients; add to the creamed mixture alternately with bananas. Spread into a greased 13-in. x 9-in. x 2-in. baking pan. Top with cranberry sauce.

In a small bowl, combine brown sugar, pecans and flour; stir in butter. Sprinkle over cranberries.

Bake at 350 degrees F for 45-50 minutes or until a toothpick inserted near the center comes out clean. Cool in pan on a wire rack.

Creamy Peach Coffee Cake

Ingredients

- 2 1/4 cups all-purpose flour 3/4 cup sugar
- 3/4 cup cold butter
- 3/4 cup sour cream
- 1/2 teaspoon baking powder
- 1/2 teaspoon baking soda
- 1 egg
- 1 teaspoon almond extract FILLING:
- 1 (8 ounce) package cream cheese, softened
- 1/4 cup sugar 1 egg
- 3/4 cup peach preserves
- 1/2 cup sliced almonds

Directions

In a mixing bowl, combine the flour and sugar; cut in butter until mixture resembles coarse crumbs. Set aside 1 cup for topping. To the remaining crumb mixture, add the sour cream, baking powder, baking soda, egg and extract; beat until blended. Press onto the bottom and 2 in. up the sides of a greased 9-in. springform pan.

In a small mixing bowl, combine the cream cheese, sugar and egg. Spoon into prepared crust. Top with preserves. Sprinkle with reserved crumb mixture; top with almonds. Place pan on a baking sheet. Bake at 350 degrees F for 45-50 minutes or until filling is set and crust is golden brown. Cool on a wire rack for 15 minutes. Carefully run a knife around edge of the pan to loosen; remove sides of pan. Cool for 1-1/2 hours before slicing. Store in the refrigerator.

Ginger-Pear Coffee Cake

Ingredients

- 1 (.25 ounce) package active dry yeast
- 1/4 cup warm water (105 degrees to 115 degrees)
- 1 cup warm buttermilk (105 to 115 degrees F)
- 1/4 cup sugar
- 2 tablespoons butter or stick margarine, melted
- 1 teaspoon salt
- 3 cups all-purpose flour FILLING:
- 1 1/2 cups diced peeled fresh pears
- 1/2 cup raisins
- 1/3 cup chopped walnuts
- 1 tablespoon ground cinnamon 1/2 teaspoon ground ginger
- 1/2 teaspoon grated lemon peel 1/4 teaspoon ground cloves
- 1 tablespoon butter or stick margarine, softened
- 1/4 cup sugar
- 1 egg, lightly beaten GLAZE:
- 1 cup confectioners' sugar
- 1/4 teaspoon vanilla extract
- 3 teaspoons milk

Directions

In a mixing bowl, dissolve yeast in warm water. Add buttermilk, sugar, butter, salt and 1-1/2 cups flour. Beat in just until moistened. Add egg; beat for 2 minutes. Stir in enough remaining flour to form a soft dough. Turn onto a lightly floured surface; knead until smooth and elastic, about 6-8 minutes.

Place in a bowl coated with nonstick cooking spray, turning once to coat top. Cover and let rise in a warm place until doubled, about 1 hour. For filling, combine the first seven filling ingredients. Punch dough down.

Turn onto a lightly floured surface. Roll into a 16-in. x 9-in. rectangle. Spread butter over dough. Sprinkle pear mixture to within 1/2 in. of edges. Sprinkle with sugar.

Roll up jelly-roll style starting with long side; pinch seems to seal. Place seam side down on a baking sheet coated with nonstick cooking spray. Pinch ends together to form a ring.

With scissors, cut from outside edge to two-thirds of the way toward center of ring at 1-in. intervals. Separate strips slightly; twist to allow filling to show.

Cover and let rise in a warm place until doubled, about 50 minutes. Brush dough with egg. Bake at 375 degrees F for 20-25 minutes or until golden brown. Cool on a wire rack.

For glaze, combine confectioners' sugar, vanilla and enough milk to achieve drizzling consistency. Drizzle over ring.

Cinnamon Coffee Frosting

Ingredients

- 1 teaspoon instant coffee granules 1/2 teaspoon ground cinnamon
- 1 pinch salt
- 1 teaspoon vanilla extract
- 1/2 cup butter, softened
- 3 cups confectioners' sugar 1/3 cup milk

Directions

In a small bowl, mash instant coffee with the back of a spoon until powdery. Stir in cinnamon and salt. In a large bowl, beat the butter until smooth, then stir in spice mixture and vanilla.

Alternately beat in confectioners' sugar and milk until desired consistency is achieved.

Coffee Shortbread Cookies

Ingredients

- 1/2 cup finely ground almonds
- 1 1/4 cups sifted all-purpose flour 3/4 cup confectioners' sugar
- 2 tablespoons instant coffee powder
- 3/4 cup butter, softened
- 1/3 cup granulated sugar for decoration

Directions

In large bowl combine almonds, flour, confectioners' sugarand coffee. Cut in the butter and mix together until well blended. Shape dough into a ball, wrap in foil or plastic and refrigerate for at least half an hour.

On lightly floured surface roll chilled dough to about 1/4 inch thickness. Cut with 2 inch cookie cutter. Place cookies 1 inch apart on ungreased cookie sheet and sprinkle tops with granulated sugar.

Bake 10-12 minutes in a preheated 350 degrees F (175 degrees C) oven or until edges are just firm. Remove from sheet. Cool cookies on wire rack.

Baileys® Iced Coffee

Ingredients

- 3 1/2 ounces Baileys Original Irish Cream
- 7 ounces freshly-brewed coffee

Directions

Brew coffee and allow to coolPour Baileys and coffee into a tall, ice-filled glass Stir and enjoy!

Spiced Coffee with Cream

Ingredients

- 1/4 cup evaporated milk
- 2 1/4 teaspoons Confectioners' sugar
- 1/4 teaspoon ground cinnamon 1/8 teaspoon vanilla extract
- 1 cup hot, strong brewed coffee ground nutmeg
- 2 cinnamon sticks

Directions

Pour milk into a small mixing bowl; place mixer beaters in the bowl. Cover and freeze for 30 minutes or until ice crystals begin to form.

Add the sugar, cinnamon and vanilla; beat until thick and fluffy. Pour about 1/2 cup into each cup.

Add coffee; sprinkle with nutmeg. Serve immediately; garnish with cinnamon sticks if desired.

Luscious Lemon Coffee Cake

Ingredients

- TOPPING:
- 1 cup chopped walnuts 1/2 cup sugar
- 2 teaspoons ground cinnamon CAKE:
- 1 (18.25 ounce) package yellow cake mix with pudding
- 1 (3.4 ounce) package instant lemon pudding mix
- 1 cup sour cream
- 4 eggs, lightly beaten
- 1/2 cup vegetable oil

Directions

Combine topping ingredients and set aside. In a mixing bowl, combine cake and pudding mixes, sour cream, eggs and oil. Mix on medium speed for 2 minutes. Pour into a greased 13-in. x 9-in. x 2-in. baking pan. Sprinkle half of the topping over batter.

Spoon remaining batter over topping and spread evenly. Sprinkle with remaining topping.

Bake at 350 degrees F for 30-35 minutes or until cake tests done.

Cinnamon Nut Coffee Cake

Ingredients

- 1 1/2 cups all-purpose flour
- 1 cup sugar
- 2 teaspoons baking powder 1/4 teaspoon salt
- 1/4 cup butter or margarine, softened
- 2 eggs, beaten 1/2 cup milk
- 1 teaspoon vanilla extract TOPPING:
- 1 cup chopped walnuts
- 1 cup packed brown sugar
- 2 tablespoons all-purpose flour
- 2 teaspoons ground cinnamon
- 2 tablespoons butter or margarine, melted

Directions

In a mixing bowl, combine flour, sugar, baking powder and salt. Stir in butter, eggs, milk and vanilla; set aside.

Combine all topping ingredients. Spread half the batter into a greased 12-in. x 8-in. x 2- in. baking pan.

Sprinkle with half of the topping. Carefully spread remaining batter over topping, then sprinkle with remaining topping.

Bake at 375 degrees F for 25-30 minutes or until cake tests done.

Coffee Date Bread

Ingredients

- 1 cup chopped pitted dates
- 1 teaspoon baking soda
- 1 cup strong brewed coffee
- 2 tablespoons butter, softened
- 1 cup white sugar
- 1 egg
- 1 teaspoon vanilla extract
- 1 1/2 cups all-purpose flour
- 1 teaspoon salt
- 1 cup chopped pecans

Directions

Preheat the oven to 350 degrees F (175 degrees C).

Grease an 8x4 inch loaf pan, and line the bottom of the pan with archment paper.

Place the dates in a small bowl, and sprinkle the baking soda over.

Heat coffee to boiling, and pour over the dates and soda. Set aside. In a medium bowl, mix together the butter, sugar and egg until well blended. Stir in vanilla. Blend in the flour and salt, then fold in the pecans and date mixture. Transfer the batter to the prepared loaf pan.

Bake for 1 hour in the preheated oven, or until the top of the loaf springs back when lightly touched. Let stand for 5 minutes before removing from pan.

Peel off paper, and allow to cool on a wire rack.

Coffee Delight

Ingredients

- 5 scoops vanilla ice cream
- 1/3 cup milk
- 1 teaspoon instant coffee granules
- 5 cubes ice

Directions

In a blender, combine ice cream, milk, instant coffee and ice. Blend until smooth. Pour into glasses and serve.

Coffee Shake

Ingredients

- 1 teaspoon instant coffee granules
- 3/4 cup milk
- 1 teaspoon vanilla extract
- teaspoons white sugar, or to taste
- 6 ice cubes 2 teaspoons chocolate syrup (optional)

Directions

Combine the instant coffee, milk, vanilla extract, sugar, ice, and chocolate syrup in a blender; blend until smooth.

Iced Coffee Syrup

Ingredients

- 1/4 cup instant coffee granules
- 2 cups hot water
- 1 (14 ounce) can sweetened condensed milk

Directions

Combine the instant coffee granules with the hot water and stir until dissolved. Stir in the condensed milk.

Store in an airtight container or jar and refrigerate, until ready to use.

Lightning Source UK Ltd.
Milton Keynes UK
UKHW020637100621
385271UK00011B/666